MY STORY TIME.

THE MAGICIAN

TELMA GUIMARÃES &
VIVIANE MARQUES

Illustrated by Enrico Marchi

Editora Saraiva

"HI, HOW ARE YOU?
I AM MR. JONES.
I'M THE MAGICIAN."

"LOOK!
THERE IS NOTHING
INSIDE THIS HAT."

"PLEASE, HELP ME HERE!
LET'S SAY THE FIRST MAGIC
WORDS... HOCUS POCUS.
COME ON, EVERYBODY
REPEAT!
HOCUS POCUS!"

"OH MAGIC HAT,
GIVE ME A PARROT!"

HOCUS POCUS

"OH NO! I'M SORRY!

THERE IS NOT A **PARROT**.

THERE ARE **CARROTS** IN THE HAT."

"I'M SORRY! I THINK WE SAID THE WRONG MAGIC WORDS. LET'S TRY AGAIN.

LET'S SAY THE WORDS **PRESTO CHENGO!** IT WILL WORK! COME ON, EVERYBODY REPEAT!"

PRESTO CHENGO

"ONE, TWO, THREE...
AND HERE IT COMES!
OH, NO! A CARROT CAKE!

I AM SO SORRY! THERE IS
NOT A **PARROT** HERE!
THERE IS A **CARROT**
CAKE INSTEAD! DO YOU
WANT A PIECE OF IT?"

"LET'S TRY ANOTHER
MAGIC TRICK.
WHAT DO YOU THINK?
MAYBE A FROG NOW...
DO YOU WANT A FROG?"

YES, WE DO!

"THESE NEXT MAGIC
WORDS ALWAYS
WORK FOR ME!
SIMSALABIM,
I NEED A FROG
TO BE SEEN!"

SIMSALABIM

"OH NO.
SOMETHING WENT WRONG!
A **HOT DOG**.
BUT I ASKED FOR A **FROG**!
I'M NOT HUNGRY! BUT IT
LOOKS DELICIOUS."

"I HAVE AN IDEA! ARE YOU HUNGRY? LET'S SAY THE MAGIC WORD AGAIN: **SIMSALABIM**."

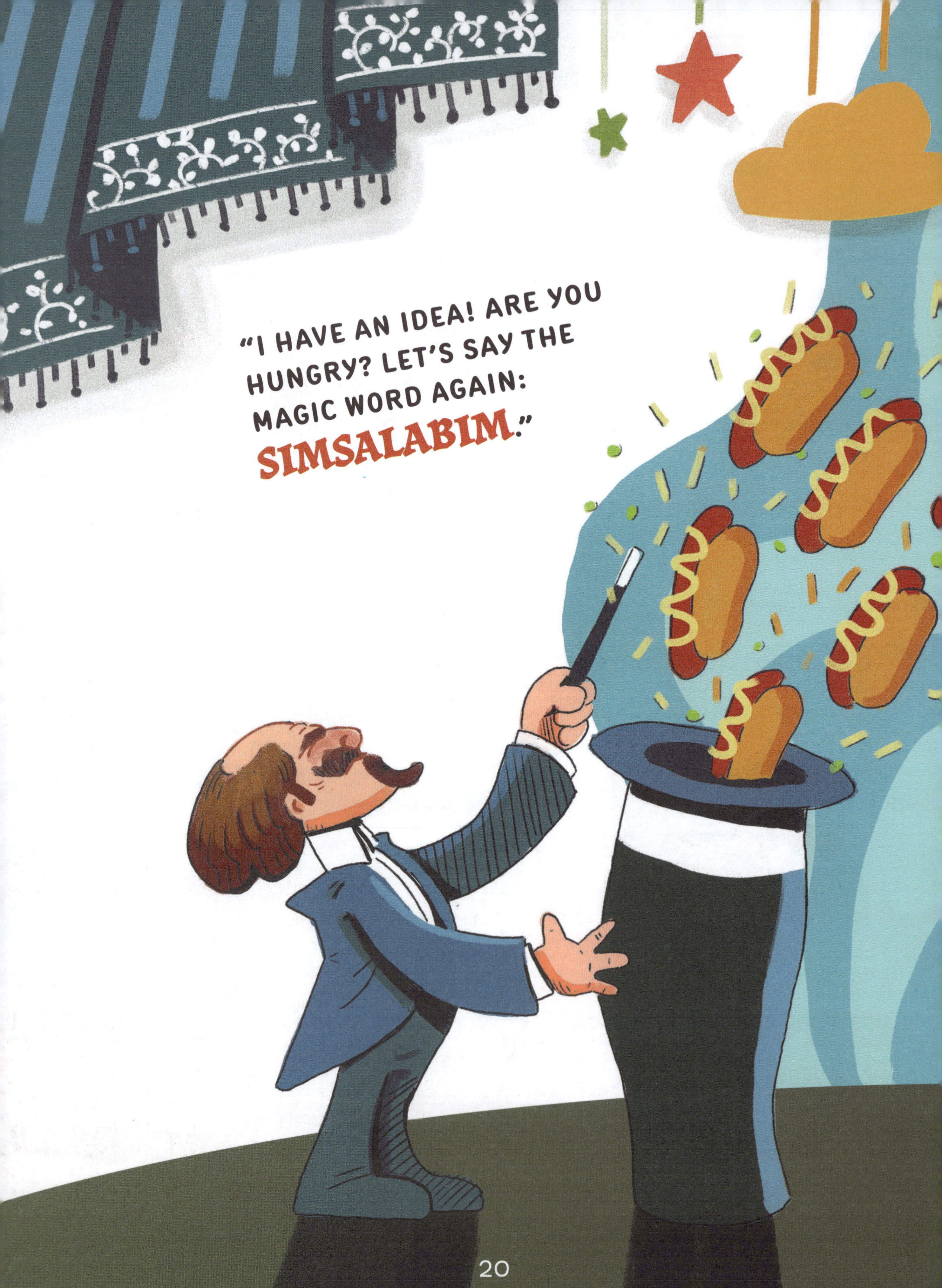

SIMSALABIM

"BUT WHERE IS THE FROG, MR. JONES?"

"I'M SO SORRY! I DON'T KNOW WHAT TO DO! HMMM, MAYBE MY SPECIAL MAGIC WORDS CAN HELP ME!"

I WANT TO
SEE A FROG!

"THAT'S IT! LET'S USE THE SPECIAL MAGIC WORDS!

FREAK-A FREAK-A BOO!

REPEAT WITH ME!"

FREAK-A
FREAK-A
BOO

"LET'S SEE WHAT
IS IN THE HAT!
A **RAT**?
A **CAT**?
WHAT IS THE PROBLEM
WITH THIS **HAT**?"

THE KIDS LOVE
THE MAGICIAN.
HE IS FUNNY!

"I'M GOING TO TRY ANOTHER MAGIC TRICK. LET'S REPEAT THE WORDS:

IZZY WIZZY, LET'S GET BUSY!

LET'S ASK FOR A **MONKEY**."

IZZY WIZZY, LET'S GET BUSY!

"A **TURKEY**! I'M SORRY!" MR. JONES IS SURPRISED. THE AUDIENCE IS LAUGHING.

"MAYBE MY PROBLEM IS MY MAGIC WAND! LET ME CHECK!"

"LET'S TRY A **MASK**.
OH NO, A **DESK**!

A **TOMATO**?
OH NO, A **POTATO**!

A **CAKE**?
OH NO, A **MILK SHAKE**!

A **LETTER**?
OH NO, A **SWEATER**!"

"LOOK!
THE PARROT IS
ON THE DESK!

THE CAKE IS
MADE OF POTATO!

THE MONKEY IS
DRINKING THE MILKSHAKE.

THE FROG IS
WEARING THE SWEATER."

MR. JONES IS A REAL FUNNY MAGICIAN

THE AUTHORS

My name is Telma Guimarães. I was born in Marília, São Paulo. When I was a teenager, I took an Exchange program in Covington, Georgia. It was a wonderful experience. I graduated with a bachelor degree in Languages, English and Literature at UNESP. I moved to Campinas and then I started teaching English. I have three children and I loved telling stories to my kids. Many of the stories were created by me.

My heart was always full of joy when I sat on my chair and thought about children, animals, nature and so on. So, I gave up teaching and tried to reach my goal: to be an author. Here I am. Viviane is a friend of mine, and now, my partner. We get along very well. We are always happy!

I'm Viviane Marques. I was born in a small town called Rafard, São Paulo, but I've lived in Campinas since I was a baby. I decided to be an English Teacher when I was in high school. I studied Languages at PUC-Campinas. After that, I studied Psychopedagogy and I also took a pronunciation course in Harvard, Boston, Massachusetts. I have been an English Teacher for students of different ages: from kindergarten to college.

I enjoy telling my family (my husband, a son, a daughter and a dog) the stories that I tell in my classes and new ones too. The story in this book is a nice example of that. They have enjoyed it a lot. I hope you guys will too. My dear friend Telma and I are so happy to share this one with you.

Quadro Europeu Comum de Referência para Línguas (CEFR)

A1 A2 B1 B2 C1 C2

The Magician

Presidência Mario Ghio Júnior

Vice-presidência de educação digital Camila Montero Vaz Cardoso

Direção editorial Lidiane Vivaldini Olo

Gerência editorial Julio Cesar Augustus de Paula Santos

Coordenação editorial Laura Vecchioli do Prado

Aprendizagem digital Renata Galdino (ger.), Beatriz de Almeida Pinto Rodrigues da Costa (coord. Experiência de Aprendizagem), Carla Isabel Ferreira Reis (coord. Produção Multimídia), Daniella dos Santos Di Nubila (coord. Produção Digital), Rogerio Fabio Alves (coord. Publicação), Vanessa Tavares Menezes de Souza (coord. Design Digital)

Planejamento, controle de produção e indicadores Flávio Matuguma (ger.), Juliana Batista (coord.) e Jayne Ruas (analista)

Edição Instituto Parole

Revisão Ray Shoulder e Maria Claudia Franchi

Ilustração, projeto gráfico e diagramação Enrico Esposito Marchi

Capa Thatiana Kalaes

Dados Internacionais de Catalogação na Publicação (CIP)

Guimarães, Telma
The Magician / Telma Guimarães, Viviane Marques ; ilustrações de Enrico Marchi. -- 1. ed. – São Paulo : Saraiva, 2022.

ISBN 978-65-5867-110-7

1. Literatura infantojuvenil - Língua Inglesa I. Título II. Marques, Viviane III. Marchi, Enrico

22-5201 CDD 028.5

Angélica Ilacqua - CRB-8/7057

CL: 531267

CAE: 795105

2022

1ª edição

1ª tiragem

Impressão e acabamento: Gráfica Elyon

Saraiva

Direitos desta edição cedidos à Somos Sistemas de Ensino S.A.

Av. Paulista, 901, Bela Vista – São Paulo – SP – CEP 01310-200

Tel.: (0xx11) 4003-3061

Conheça o nosso portal de literatura Coletivo Leitor: www.coletivoleitor.com.br

Este livro foi composto nas fontes *Herb JAF*, *Pinecone MVB*
e *Grenadine MVB* e impresso sobre papel off set 90 g/m2.